Poetry
34562

The Clearing

David Keplinger

New Issues Poetry & Prose

A Green Rose Book

New Issues Poetry & Prose
The College of Arts and Sciences
Western Michigan University
Kalamazoo, Michigan 49008

An Inland Seas Poetry Book

 Inland Seas poetry books are supported by a grant from The Michigan Council for Arts and Cultural Affairs.

Copyright © 2005 by David Keplinger. All rights reserved.
Printed in the United States of America.

First Edition, 2005.

ISBN   1-930974-51-5 (paperbound)

Library of Congress Cataloging-in-Publication Data:
Keplinger, David
The Clearing/David Keplinger
Library of Congress Control Number: 2004116691

Editors	Herbert Scott, Lisa Lishman
Designer	Jenni Martin
Art Director	Tricia Hennessy
Production Manager	Paul Sizer
	The Design Center, Department of Art
	College of Fine Arts
	Western Michigan University

The Clearing

David Keplinger

New Issues

 Western Michigan University

Also by David Keplinger

The Rose Inside

for my teachers

Contents

    View from Outside   5

I.

Waking on the Pribor Train, Near Freud's Birthplace   9
Death Mask of John Keats   10
Correspondences   11
Elegy for the Precious Time Before Dinner   14
Instructions for the Lost   15
The Sun   16
Birth Mask   17
The Birth of Tragedy   18
Breast Exam   19
Portrait of a Woman   20
Persistence   21
Clear Seeing   22
Pig Slaughter   23
For William Blake. At Christmastime.   24
Cortez Arrives at San Juan de Ulloa   25
Sleep   26
The Only Story   27
Received Legends   28
Barber Shop: Rue de Rivoli   29
Clocks Kept Upside Down to Stay Awake   30
Icarus, After Matisse   31
Towards a Reconciliation with Disorder   33

II.

Basic Training   37
Classical Landscape   39
North   40
Recanting on His Deathbed, Darwin Remembers
    the Island of Chiloe   41
The Birth of Comedy   43
Krasna, Recollected   44
Three Visions of the Peril of Art   45
Late Realism   46
Robert Frost   47
The Twins Conjoined at the Head Receive Holy
    Communion at Corpus Christi Church   48
Goodman Brown in Decrepitude   49
Side Work   50
Mummified Roman Soldier in the Egyptian Exhibit   51

Lines for the Early Surrender of John Donne's Life	52
The Conditions	53
Resolve	54
Philadelphia, 1976	55
Towards a Reconciliation with Order	56

III.

Justice	61
The Joke	62
The Sea	63
Further Entries from the Notebook of Anton Chekhov	64
"Departure's Particular Handkerchief"	73
Attractions	74
The Birth of Melodrama	76
Max Jacob at Abbey St. Benoit-sur-Loire	77
Without	78
Our Secret Icarus Is	79
Lorca's Passport	80
Mother, Father	81
View from Inside	82
Notes	85

View from Outside

He didn't want the EKG. He didn't want
To know. But the nurse attached
Its greasy patches to his chest to read.
From which all things spray violent
And out, there is a point of singularity.
In Michelangelo's sculpture of the heart,
For instance, the heart wears the costume
Of David's body. In the eyes of the Judean
There is no fear of what the heart has made.
You are going into cardiac arrest, this nurse said.
That's when he saw the thing the other way:
Something mute sat like a stone
Inside the clenching and unclenching of his heart.
He had the stone. Only it would pay attention.

I.

*"He who sees the infinite in all things sees God.
He who sees the ratio sees only himself."*
—William Blake

Waking on the Pribor Train, Near Freud's Birthplace

I hear before I see.
Halfway through the rain-wet
Fields of Pribor in winter,
Some distant, barking dogs
Suggest the town.
I have heard tell
Of its shops with names
Predating the war
When this was a Jewish city.
I have found it all this way
Like a cup or a pocketknife
Or a hat from childhood
I thought was lost.
Illumined by the station lights
The tiny veins
Flicker behind my eyes,
And I open my eyes:
It's like floating back into the world
After prayer. The moon
Is out. The dogs are slick
And fluid in their tight, black fur.

Death Mask of John Keats

Rome, February 23 1821

No thinker's face, he is twenty-five and dead.
The artifice of nightingales, the mind,
The half-loves of his life, can't capture what's behind
This plaster forehead. But of his spirit ditties
This was being written all along: a gritty,
Sad collapse. The mask survives the young man's head.

What could any Roman know
About his hyper-critic's mind, his *animus,* the mere
Flutter of a sound against a sound, like Kingdom come?
They cast it into plaster. It does not teem.
He would have wondered at the hieroglyphic brow,
Illegible and tense. There's a man who loved his fear.

Already late in February, the famous
Roman earth kept opening; the bees would grow colossal
With alacrity and greed. Without him in the world,
The world had failed to change. What in heaven would?
His last report's a homely fossil
Ever young; the eyes shut up; ever knitted to their darknesses.

Correspondences

1. *How the Brain Emerged from Water*

Chemical, mathematical, the brain was a fish.
Go into your head to imagine it: the face,

Like it's blowing out a candle. The fins,
Invisible as sleep. Hold that kingdom in your hands:

It wriggles out. It swallows almost anything.
It stinks like its kin and its hook.

2. *How the Moth Became the Magpie*

The moth, his full beard coated with dust, knew he was dying, so what else? He began to cry. His own tears dissolved the delicate powder of his wings.

The fall proved unbearable: the moon animated on the lake, its white light flickering from disguise to disguise, and also to the grasses, bent in a great wind that carried him. This is why the magpie says, "We are carried."

He was Colossus, the acrobat, lithe, lucky, far away, flying further out. His feathers were black, were white. His feathers were blue inside the wing. He was the colors of that lake in darkness.

3. *How the Mouth Emerged from Fire*

Negative organ, the mouth is a burnt-out hole,
A tragedy worthy of fire. The tongue is the only survivor,
    deformed.

Spoiled meat locker. You yearn for the alliances, the cold
Union of the body, the oligarchies of the fingers and the toes.
And you're jealous of the crotch that seethes,

But it's you we flush with water. Because maybe you still smolder.
Maybe you taste of ashes, and you sting.

4. *How the Bat Became the Crow*

The empty hollow of an egg, bat's stomach. His skin felt sick.

You know how, under the right conditions, when a person dies in the cold, the eyes and mouth withdraw, the skin loosens like the hides of beasts?

Now the oily feathers burrowed through. Now he could hear, but with his eyes: A spider was falling out of the sky. He would never have to follow it again. Standing up he made the sound of *crow,* that God makes.

5. *How the Feet Emerged from Salt*

Though lifetimes swirl in the forever
Of these carbons, the story of the feet is brief.

I have seen how infants hold
The lick of the foot to their mouths. Succulent, delicious
Whorl of salt: an infant might like to return to you, but I do not.

6. *How the Crayfish Became the Water Strider*

The crayfish had a kingdom, a stone. He was a stoic. He had no brains to fear the dark he lived in. He lived there.

It's not difficult, reduced to this, to govern. His face was indecipherable, except for its outsider's grin. His body was hard and impenetrable. He couldn't even remember how to move.

One story goes like this. He remembered how to move. When he did, the kingdom toppled over. That's how he discovered he'd been under water. Now he moves along the surface of the water: having everything.

7. How the Heart Emerged from Air

The heart began as a point. It grazed
The soapy rims of stars. It became a straight line.
The atmosphere of earth was a scrappy land to find.

Forget the heart's a sky. Its planets are circling
To their own music, to their own math,
And they never show their work.

My own heart, my tiny savant, goodnight.
You sleep with your eyes wide open,
The skin of the body pulled over your head.

Elegy for the Precious Time Before Dinner

Along the fringe of the two known worlds
Of field, of prison yard,
Behind the house my mother and her sisters
Live in, this was years ago.

We're all still there, itinerant
As wind, the straits of corn
And prison guards who pace their impossible promontories,
And the small mouse just born into this world,
Total as a thumb.

With her sisters who are dead, my mother is a beauty
Taking the spoon
To beat the dog away from the pot,
At which they all begin to laugh.

Little beetles with a kind of Viking armor
I want to smash you, smash the spiders
Atop their pagodas
Like bad thoughts,
Smash the crazy locust that won't abandon its post.

At the house the women happily
Eye up the sauce about to boil.
I am wearing my emblematic cape.
I can fly at any moment if I want to,
But I don't.

Instructions for the Lost

Above the cellars
Lined with preserves,
In a foreign year,
Its calendar girls
Naked except for their parasols,
You may find
That you are lost.
You may listen
To the gurgle of the small
Red chimneys
Filling up with dark.
Into that dark
That sleeves
The bare branches
Like a heavy sack,
A crow will disappear, children.
Pay attention to the crow.
The windpipe
With its tiny rungs.

The Sun

Only the ascetics understood it.
To be one of them, it's said, you must
Make of yourself a sun.
The whole body on fire, that's
The way. You have to be bereft
But not a hunger to forget the world.
You have to let the summer girls
Completely pass you by. One day
You sit assembling your death
Like a tattered map, and the next
You're up there, very close
To the sun. If you can let go, those beauties
Stop instructing you to live or die.

Birth Mask

My father kept
His birth mask
In his wallet
With the pictures
Of Wisconsin,
Bad boy
Smiling back at us
From boot camp.

This other face
Was merely skin,
Skin and salt.
Whatever it was,
It was round.
It was just
The size,
He once said,
Of the inside
Of his mother's hand.
It came out white
As bacon fat.
It was yellow now
With age.

In this story
He told my mother
When they met,
The midwife
Dropped it
Down the bathroom sink:
She had to pry
Into that afterworld
Of pipes
And clogs
But got hold of it.
She fished it
With two fingers
From the
Narrow hole,
Where it had fallen.

The Birth of Tragedy

The day on which the other days were hinged,

When finally you saw you'd fucked it up,

Nothing could forgive the thing

You did that hurt the others,

Your short affair soon publicized to everyone.

What could you do? What could you do?

The small TV atop the mantle

Blabbed like in a basket in the clouds;

Its laugh tracks screamed right in your face;

Your atoms firm as decimals,

Taut in their knot.

Breast Exam

Below us, the dog has made a clearing
In the dirt and fallen fast asleep.
The sky, boundless as it seems, clambers
All the way into the window behind you.
The house is a clearing for the human world.
You lie on the bed, the mattress pressed and green.
Your hands caress the tissue down
To the ribs; they make small circles
Across each breast, one at a time. It is late summer.
The corn, like frail, miraculous cilia, wheezes
Whenever wind spears through those narrow alleys.

Portrait of a Woman

*Encaustic and gilt on a wooden panel wrapped
in linen, Romano Egyptian, 100 A.D.*

A blush of pigment skies
Into your forehead; the olive green
Of home begins to swell along the nape.
They gave you imperfections. One eye bulges, cocked
To the left. Your purple cheek
Has wilted.

In the middle of your life, in the middle of the flex
Of Roman law, you were buried,
O flawed, particular one.
When was this glance you offered?
It was painted on an ordinary
Wooden board.

We'll call you Isidora. We'll call this
Isidora's grave. They carved the name
Into the linen plaster of your mummy case.
Two thousand years have not yet brushed
The brevity of thought
Out of your face.

Persistence

Mickey's Barber Shop, 1980

Closing up shop for the night.
In the cabinet he locks
His catalogs and tonics.
He gathers the forgotten
Hats and scarves
And the newspapers
Like a stage manager.
He gathers the sounds that are left
At the end of the day.

Things had a Latin of their own,
This street, the night sky
Were luminous, once.
His secret is quieter
Than money. He waits
For the frayed, loose cuttings
Like propellers
To spin to the floor.
The widow's peaks, especially,
Take a good, long time.

Clear Seeing

Still drunk, she woke to find that all her things
Were waking too. Opening her eyes
The photographs and hanging stockings
Glared. And these things glared: the bee
On her windowsill. The pair of jeans
She'd peeled away. The scuffed, still gaping
Shoes kicked sideways on the floor. The mean
Alarm was shrill and loud and threatening . . .

She quickly muted that. Then things behaved
The way they always had. There was no reason
Anything should change. She should have
Acquiesced when last night's One
Climbed on top of her again. She kept
Her eyes away from him, like being raped.

Pig Slaughter

The house that held it
Still stinks of death. The hurdle
Worst to cross was killing.
The butcher with his butcher's gun
Arrived and got himself acquainted
With the pig. The pig has knowledge,

Too; the pig is kind or cruel
Depending; it winces like a dog
Before it's hit. The happy butcher
Slung it to the ladder standing upright
At the house, and from the neck
He sliced the dead, delicious skin.

Into a drum the life pumped.
He stirred the blood by hand. Someone
Cleaned the guts. Someone cooking barley
Stuffed it hard into the warm, blue tubes.
The rest is tenderness. The roasting of the pig
Is like no quiet I have known.

For William Blake. At Christmastime.

These angels we might see, to him
Were quite the ordinary kind. Was not his art
His life: A way to entertain the children?
A shade in which to slip his hands?
His work was in the garden with his hands,

Casting that severe, hard ground to joy.
Like any other day, he cleans a bit of universe
From his fingernails, stops to listen to the music
In the street. One trumpet, he is certain,
Is a hell beast's mouth, but lacking teeth.

Cortez Arrives at San Juan de Ulloa

He belongs to no one now.
He trims his beard with tiny golden scissors. He whittles
At his fingertips.

Each shoulder in its armor, the liquidy hollow
Of an egg. He fits his feet in stirrups.
He yanks the rotten tooth.

And this is Cortez in his boots: Lord of Fire,
Lord of Death, whose ship is burning, who spits and gives commands
Into the air,

That he is never going back; to the one wave turning
On another; to that ash heap; that boat;
That murdering sea.

Sleep

1.
He lets her sleep, so small that he could lift her up
With one little finger, like in a game he played
As a boy, *light as a feather, stiff as a board.*
He holds her hand. Her hands are bent-up claws.
Her bones are hollow flutes. They curve
As balsa underneath the surface of her skin.
Her skin is vague and papery, like sky he's driving in
Until she's just a point inside the rear view.
For her the point is this one white room.

2.
The way they have known her these years,
She turns in sleep in a dream without sound,
Without image, the myth data broken from its anchor,
Split into light that folds over light, in waves
Over and over and over. And when her children come, Where
Are you? They beg of her, What has become of you?
They take away her things. All are satisfied
And think it best. But there is money
No one knows about, dumb in rubber bands and foil.
She's hidden it where they won't find it. In the houses of her sleep.

The Only Story

The twins have grown more fascinated
With the old and wasted away,
The astonishment of death
In the decapitated head,
No matter whose.

In the vague familiarity
Of abandoned places
They are looking
For the heads of chickens
In the barn,

That petrified stare
Of which there is only one.
It begins to speak to them,
A little garbled at first.
They have their tiny slingshots just in case.

Received Legends

In one version, Oedipus remarries,
Sits at home, blind, beloved,
The dog licking his elderly foot.
Jocasta's sudden look of horror
Is a long, disentangled memory.
He had no children. He enjoys
His music, thinks how leisurely it is
Not to work. No Choragus
To bother him in counsel; no
Hermaphrodites about. The news
Is good from Corinth; the family
Is well and planning a trip
To the seaside. Laius sits in hell
Still dressed up as a gladiator king,
Complaining how he had the right
Of way. In this version, the wife
Is young and pretty, looks nothing
Like her haggard man. The smell
Of goat's milk boiling at the fire.
The texture of her face. His knowledge
Of the worst never truly sinking in.

Barber Shop: Rue de Rivoli

This world's a kind of staticky buzz,
Old barber with the courtroom sigh.

The customer with head bent low.
That boy asleep on piles of winter coats,

He's next. *Un murmure petit dans le coeur,*
His mother announces sadly.

His brothers crunch their boots outside,
Marching through the snow.

Clocks Kept Upside Down to Stay Awake

When it's over,
We'll go into the attic with the bags
Of Kathryn's gowns,
All those New Year's Eves.

We'll choose among her clothes of high occasion.
We'll choose among her good shoes
In shut-up boxes,
Tissues jammed into the mouths.

For now it's like this.
She eats, finishes a bowl
Of sweets, draws the white curtains.
This will go on for some time.

Her heart gets fat, the brain
Sits and fidgets. The face is a rag
That covers a stone.
She is either tragically young

Or comically old,
It's always changing.
We'll fit the ring back on her hand.
We'll hover in our overcoats, and go.

Icarus, After Matisse

1.
I wondered how I would drown,
Flailing my arms,
Or listening.

Why flail
With the wings
Taking on water, getting heavy,

Getting heavier, the way Zeus
Must have felt, falling
From the heavens as a swan?

Nothing can stay
Completely above the earth, above
Themselves for long.

What is semen, after all?
What swan is that?
Even the Christ,

His hands outstretched,
Or rather, hammered down,
Had to let go of everything.

2.
You taught me
To be patient
And good,

But it was for nothing;
In all of literature
It's only savages

Who earn a name.
Even you should understand
That hunger, for the ovum

The sun. Father,
You built my form,
And therefore

No offense;
I had to know
That you were

Not its source.
I wanted to experience
That ultimate sun;

My own death
Rushing towards
Itself. But that

Was much too difficult,
And finally
Did not console me.

Towards a Reconciliation with Disorder

Nothing can be described. In this
The work of art is mere forgiveness.
I knew a man whose life was irreconcilable.
We must look into the sun, he said. Let's say
The gesture of compassion is an attack
Against form, against structure, dubious
Shell in which we trust. This man was crass,
Nearly to the point of clarity. He showed me how
He fixed his mouth over a boy soldier's wound,
To save the soldier from bleeding to death.
What's one sun colliding with the others?
What's one death if it can't be everything? Anyway,
The soldier died. Forgive me, this man said.

II.

*"Were all educations practical and ornamental well
 displayed out of me, what would it amount to?"*
—Walt Whitman

Basic Training

His sits on the Greyhound bus.
Just below his window
Where the driver smokes,
The year is 1955.

He's on his way to basic training.
The father sells insurance
And has been on strike
And has time

To take his son to the station.
He has time
To make a little
Chit chat. He talks about

Some money he has earned
Selling rare coins.
He talks to his son
From the street.

The passing traffic
Shakes the Greyhound bus.
The father lights a cigarette
And gazes towards

Some small, indefinable point
On the horizon.
The son looks at it, too.
They look at it and look at it.

The son would like a cigarette.
He would like his father
To tell him what he sees.
But the father says

One more thing:
What was it? The other
Will always have to wonder,
Have to tell about,

Like this,
As the bus shoves off;
And the door closes;
The enormous wing.

Classical Landscape

When Moyer's cow got blocked,
The hole he called her rosebud
Clenched the plastic bag
That served as a rudimentary glove.
The tail was smeared with shit
He fed by handfuls from the rectum;
From the anus; opened to the width
Of his wrist. And all the sick poured out.
He called it *Christ* when he removed the arm
The way an arm draws back an arrow.

North

The saddest trains go north.
Along the aisles
Men hang in place.

They grasp the drooping wires
And try not to remember
Their loneliness.

The women sit. They wave,
They move their hands
Like through water. They clutch

Their purses and square hats.
They are so busy, they have no time
To ward off strangers.

When they come back,
All bow forward like in a prayer.
The men unclench.

The women gather their things:
The hands of children still asleep
Are heaviest.

Recanting on His Deathbed, Darwin Remembers the Island of Chiloe

> "... and they are all Christians, but it is said that they pretend to hold communion with the devil in certain caves ..."
> —*From* The Voyage of the Beagle

Almost never did I get a view as clear
As that: dormant Cordillero,
As the sun came up, without the glare
Or rain. After that, the work was slow
From plodding through the muck and scum.
I should have died before the ship turned home.

I didn't die. And never thought I would, not ever.
Even in my sicknesses, or all alone
Inside the bush, the metal taste
Of vomit in my mouth. Is a man just a brain
That thinks its soul came first?
Does he die, even if he dies for another?

November 10th, the sea was full
Of violence, and Cordillero disappeared for good.
I sat inside the Beagle with the peat
And Barking-birds: the food
Did not agree with me. The stink of sheep
And wild potato, rotting in the hull;

No wonder all the Indians were sick with worms.
They ate diseases from their quadrupeds.
They warned me how the spirits of the dead
Inhabited my specimens of birds.
They prayed in angry outbursts.
They used the Christian terms.

Once, I met them at the cave
Where they held service
And, by some trick of fire, I observed
A man transformed into a kind of bird
I couldn't name. Nature works by her devices;
Where was her logic then? What shall I believe?

The hot volcano rumbled, out of sight. Immediately,
The bird became a man again. And I returned to all
My specimens and notebooks on the Beagle,
The million years of history to wrestle,
And my four sad, nomadic walls.
And the future. And the apocalyptic sea.

The Birth of Comedy

Someone placed a kick-me sign
On Oedipus, his first night in the wild.

Clumps of mushrooms snickered in the wings.
The tiny beasts

Watched him from their hiding places,
Clutching at their sides.

It was Crow, of course,
Who kicked him first. "Take that,"

Said Crow, as the forest broke out laughing,
"Because you had to be the good one. The heavy."

Krasna, Recollected

Old snow melts
Over latticework
And shutters,
And the rooftops of Krasna
Come back.
They come back
And the man
Who sells eggs
And is dim
Comes back
With his boxes
And his samples
In sandwich bags,
The hovering yolks.
Last night
He says
When he thought of his father
Who lies buried
With the red candles
In Krasna,
He nearly understood.
He made the coffee
On the small
Clay oven
With the open fire.
He listened to the bad news
On the wooden radio.
He turned the
Enormous dial
From communist times.
He sang, "It matters;
It doesn't matter."
He fell asleep
To the snow
He says
And the silent chickens
In their coops
And the sound
Of his own scrubbing,
Muscular and dense,
Bent over
The kitchen floor.

Three Visions of the Peril of Art

1. *Childhood Home of Smetana*

The snowed-over tracks carried us
Like Providence. We lived in an occupied country
Before the wars. We were passing through his little town.
Smetana the Deaf once held rapt
Sudetan and Jew alike; they crowded in to hear him
At the National House. He called his music "My Land."
The snow and faces in the station hovered
Over the bags on the platform. Then I was falling back asleep.
I dreamed of blaring sound that swallowed everything.

2. *Brueghel's "Peasant Wedding"*

Because the groom is absent,
Looker, you must be her groom. You are the missing
Flash of life, a ghost, the happy citizen of Flanders.
Go to this clearing in the woods
Where the lapis is hidden, and locusts
Burst their prisons. The woman was married
In an overwhelming stench of sugar
And beer. She wears a crown of peacock feathers,
A gown the color of shoes.

3. *This Story's Mine about My Mother*

"I want to suffer my own suffering
And die my own death," my mother wrote
Into a book of poems I once gave her.
When I discovered them,
I felt those lines more brutally
Than any in the book. She told me once
And I believe her
That whatever I make with my own hands
Is mine. The earth is sad and right, she also said.

Late Realism

Love wants to be sadness. Therefore,
The land cannot be saved. The farmers
Must resort to ardent prayer. In their cornfields,
A Bronze Age armor hardens
On the stalks. The tassels will not fight.

Consider the woman who sparked
A forest fire that spread a hundred miles:
She was a ranger burning letters from a former love.
That she burned them out of love
Did not save the land. The land cannot
Be saved by us. It doesn't need the past.

Robert Frost

I rediscovered Frost at thirty-three.
He talked to me just like my father did.
I had the sense of Frost well memorized
By thirty-three. Another year and all
The meanings changed. Dear father at that age,
Made holy by a bulb in our garage,
You mend the arrows I have broken. You glue
The broken parts; you fix them in your hands
Like this, two fists. With twine you wrap each
Fracture so the glue will hold. I used to say:
I take them to the trash to hide my shame.
Enough. The glue holds well. The meanings give.
The sturdy arrows fly where I command.

The Twins Conjoined at the Head Receive Their First Holy Communion at Corpus Christi Church

Father Henry Funk
Made it a point
To bless them right to left.

Our society of eyes,
The day and its heat,
It was all held together

By an orderly longing.
With their hands the twins
Formed two palettes.

The One is not one,
We who witnessed this
Would tell.

Goodman Brown in Decrepitude

It might have been too effortless to bend,
Return to Faith, their sober pew. He wouldn't
Soften or forgive, if just to get some sleep.

He fretted down to bones and hair and teeth,
To such a state that no one knew him anymore,
Not even Faith, who'd had all she could bear.

Between his legs a hoary patch had grown.
The marriage failed. In his sleeping gown
He spit on Salem village, drew the spit

Up in his mouth for all the years of spite,
And even when he died, he was bitching.
A little fly was all that came to fetch him.

Side Work

Great things begin
In the periphery.
Meanwhile my father

Works third shift
At the mustard plant.
He's around my age.

He's finished
For the night.
He revs his truck,

Waiting for the heat.
The ladder shakes
In its rack on top.

The heat is dusty,
Coming on. All this
Can happen

Without us, just
Out of view:
It's almost morning.

The smallest tools
Begin to shudder now,
In their boxes.

Mummified Roman Soldier in the Egyptian Exhibit

The soldier's face recorded on the head
Of his sarcophagus, made mural
Under glass. I found him in the basement
With the ordinary vats for beer
And parlor games that entertain
The dead. His coffin locked away
The soft cream features
Of his face. He died
And found his way into this holy care.

How must it be, his service in the heaven
Of the occupied? Buried in his
Cartonnage, perfumed, and left to dry,
His foreign birth is mystery. His death
The story of the soldier in Algiers.
The heavy lidded eyes as firm
And flexible as reeds. The curve
Of mandible relaxes. Whoever left
Their native land would know
His kind: unleavened hosts, the heart,
The brain, discarded, dissolved in light.
Whoever served, would apprehend
This hollowed place prepared for him.

Lines for the Early Surrender of John Donne's Life

The clutter of the self—when he was still
A boy in London at the Sunday mass,
A Catholic boy, marshaled to the cross
To be confirmed—he knew that it was all
No more than mystery, and the veil
Of human shame. But when the bishop stooped
And slapped his face, he shook, he dropped
Into a kind of cosmic hole.
It emanated from the heart of Christ.
Down into the gullet of that beast
He fell, and later, as a man in crisis
He'd remember it. He longed to free
The battered heart of Christ where it was nailed.
Because the hole could swallow him, he kneeled.

The Conditions

> *"In order to arrive at what you are not*
> *You must go through the way in which you are not."*
> —Eliot, "East Coker"

1 Solomanovic has nightmares of not drowning.

2 Colored flowers pass his face under water, and when they touch him there's a static charge.

3 There's a static charge and the urge to float, and the urge to go all the way down to the bottom, he said.

4 In the dream he dives from the water into air and wakes up sobbing.

5 In the camps he was a child.

6 To stay alive he curtsied for his guards.

7 There were other children who played games and sang religious songs, this Solomanovic said.

8 Oh but if you're smart, he said, You're more careful.

Resolve

Because he had to pay
For his daughters'
Fanned out gowns,
My grandfather
Cut hair at night.

The light was bad.
The customer sat
In his backwards cape
And watched himself in the mirror.
And so did my thin grandfather.

He scraped the razor
Carefully down the nape.
Like the dead who long
For their physical bodies,
Did my grandfather

Long for something too?
With talc he mopped
The barbered neck.
He had to hold his face
Up close, to help this man.

Philadelphia, 1976

The flourish of the General
With sword and horse, unemotional
And terse, is the work of unknowns
Who made the face from steel
For the courtyard of the hall.
They dressed us up in knickers
To go and see, little revolutionaries
From Mrs. Watson's second grade,
Far from my mother and the suburbs.
Before the judge, the guide said,
The convicted man would wait
Inside an iron gate where he was tied
And made to speak when spoken to.
We did exactly as they said.
We sat along the floor. We sat
In perfect rows. Tim Gordon slid
His hyperactive elbow
Between the iron bars
And got it stuck. Mrs. Watson
Tugged him free. Then we went
For lunches with the statue and his
Angry horse, his sword thrust out
Like a terrible reverted crucifix, merely
Jabbing upwards towards the sky.

Towards a Reconciliation with Order

When we got caught and it came to an end,
I went comparing everyone to you.
I looked around. No one ever could.
If the outcome of reversal's little show
Is wisdom, wisdom's part is cruel.
We had our high romance. On campus
We had snow, though it was spring. To all
That's beautiful and good some ugliness
Must come. The motel radio was playing
"Night in Berkeley Square." The knock arrived.
That other soul. He asked to come inside.
I took his ice-wet coat. There's a saying,
"Being sensible is always for the best."
Here's what it means: I was the ugliness.

III.

"Let us leave theories there and return to here's hear."
—James Joyce

Justice

The lessons of my childhood faded.
There was no justice in anything human.
I left my shoes untied, walked around in a slump.

I played a game that solicited answers
To the questions my ancestors wrote in their copybooks:
Who is my rival? Who is my confidant?

How many servants will I have?
My birth date and year were already figuring me
To live and fail and disappear.

At night I rode a rocking horse with human hair,
Whose eyes were human, too. My cowlicks,
Slicked from my mother's hand, would not behave and stay down.

The Joke

When they searched,
The doctors heard
A snapping finger

In my brain,
A catchy
Original tune.

The brain is made
Of water, sugar,
Fatty acids, partial

Especially to fish.
It's starved, delirious,
Can't remember who it is.

Who's there?
The doctors asked.
They never got their answer.

"Knock, Knock,"
Was all that I
Or anyone could hear.

The Sea

It suits me fine.
Because I smashed
The stone against its head,
The manta ray's
Lips and belly split,
Bloody.

I killed the thing and left it.
The scavengers who came,
They didn't care
How I had found it on the beach,
How it had galloped
Out of the sea.

I smashed the head,
And out came the oily heart instead.
The wings were ferocious.
The mouth's
White lips
Moved filthily.

You can't use reason.
I had my own small portion
Of somethingness to defend.
But all I've eaten
Turns into husks
Since then.

Further Entries from the Notebook of Anton Chekhov

A historian: "The whole adventure didn't even happen to me. It's not my story. Look to that hill. Where the old school had been, a new school was built. Where the other children had played, these children wore masks and sang and danced. Like you, I have heard about the other children: how only their jaws were discovered."

From the cloakroom a woman appeared, carrying his false leg. She gave it to the man who had fallen. "We're just like a puppet theater," he said, pretending to beat her with the leg.

"I refute it thus," a certain scholar said, upon hearing that the stone does not exist. He kicked it; he broke his toe on that mystery. The toe was crushed inside his boot like chalk.

For him, there is a heavy burden to be whole. First, he must become a nothing. A hotel room: he and his lover fast asleep. Is the snow suddenly worse? Is it her husband who bangs on the door? He will have to rise to ask the banging in. The night is cold and he is naked as he carefully lifts the bolt.

He would not go to sleep until his father came home. To stay awake the boy would review the faces on the obsolete coins in his collection. In the dark he could name the date and worth by the wear on the face. Other contents of the box he preferred not to touch: the cicada's white thorax that had flinched for a day, the knife his father gave him. His father had told him to keep the knife: it having belonged to someone who was dead.

Years before his career in economics, P. was a very resistant child. One night, he was unfairly sent to bed. They came and turned out all the lights. One half-hearted cricket started up. He had no use for it. The sun still hadn't set: he had no use for it.

They are discussing the interior of the apple. The Admiral proclaims it "a darkness and a whiteness at the same time." The other guests constantly laugh at him. He has spent so many years at sea he can no longer walk without holding onto things.

A clairvoyant: "I'm bored with the future. My great love is the past. I'm not sure of anything that's ever happened."

As proof he showed us his photographs of restaurants, the blurry figures at their meals. In one of these, someone playing a violin. The playing arm appeared to be longer than the other. The face of a waiter was a splotch, his eyes unreadable. "You see?" this man insisted, "Nothing holds still in our age."

"Departure's Particular Handkerchief"

*Photograph of Lorca with Angel del Rio,
Sent to Grenada from Bushnellsville, NY, 1929*

Angel appears much older than I.
See what getting married will do?
Here at the steps of our cabin

We are far from any city. But at night
We hear the screams
At Coney Island, the workmen building

Skyscrapers, the faint stamp of heels
On dance floors. Actually, dear family,
The country life is just like home.

Angel is turning my poems into English.
He says that I am very great; he cups
My hand in his and says,

"You are very great." His eyes are old.
I would rather stay happy and young.
My impossible hair is no different here.

I know now, even American children
Adore me. Little Helen and Stanton
Take me on my walks; they are like

Cabbage hearts, so small and tough.
We have no lemon trees. We have
A phonograph, the songs are in English,

But I am learning words. The voices
Skirl into my room in operatic coils.
They sound just like the dead, they are so sad.

Why must we ever grow old, suffer
And die? Tonight I held my handkerchief
At arm's length, to lead those voices.

I waved as if to orchestrate it all.

Attractions

1. *Magic Show*

My lovely assistant gave me no credit.
She quit me. That's how I got myself

So bloody, cutting myself in half,
How the colored handkerchiefs became stuck

That time in my throat. The audience was yawning.
They wanted their money back. They were pulling

Colored handkerchiefs from their mouths. Tada, they said.

2. *High Wire Act*

Hand, our oaths took you. The hand in oath
Is Roman. The courtroom breathed its Latin sigh.

Let us hone that art. Let the people who are bad
Admit they're bad for you alone, unbending hand.

In the jury box we sat. The trial dragged.
The man who hit the woman accepted he had hit the woman.

Walking from the stand back to his seat, he faltered once.

3. *Slot Machine*

The icons were the twelve apostles.
Venerable systems of twelve,

I had a little cash to spare. When I put my money in,
And I pulled down on the lever,

The faces blurred. The faces blurred,
That's the whole story.

Triple Judas was the jackpot, spilling down all over.

4. *Tiniest Man in the World*

Look, my head is where my prick should be.
The only way to meet me is by looking down.

How small am I? In that long
Correspondence with your archetype,

My writing had a foreign accent. I'm so tiny,
Your loopy cursive hurt my ears.

You were Rapunzel in a far off tower, was our understanding.

5. *Under the Big Top*

You had the Great Chain of Being
For imaginary friends. At the very top,

An angel was a summer dress, beating on its clothespins.
At bottom, you had your ticks and saints.

You had your coliseums; you made a circle with your hands.
When your hands assumed the classical shapes,

Anything in armor sought you there.

6. *Hall of Mirrors*

The woods, and the lake, and the last
Few sunfish retreat into sleeves of dusk.

One moon breaks to pieces in the house,
Across the mother's plastic flowers.

One moon is in the water. One is in the sky
As heaven's ear. The mother's at her science in the mirror.

The father's got some work to do: a hammer in his fist.

The Birth of Melodrama

The reformed church at night with snow falling
Over its wooden steeples.

Oh you there, walking with a bellyful of carp and
Picking the reed-like bones from your teeth,

You are just a sated man walking, a true thing, like evening, like snow,
Its secret, acrobatic rhythm, its effortless design, its one event

Turning on another. The church is silent. It is full
Of blown-out candles. There can be no hope. There is no way

You will know yourself. As in this dream, in which the goddess
Appears to you, with her box and the single bat inside,

The bat flies upward crazily, satisfied at last.

Max Jacob at Abbey St. Benoit-sur-Loire

The poem grabs him by the nape:
The sullen French, their howitzers' largess
Somewhere near Petite Pierre, a passage
Like the horrors of his sleep.
Fey and inattentive at the abbey,
He twiddles in his pin-stripe with the monks.
At night he fills the heat-thick pages of his book.
He kneads his mound of bread all day.
He knows a garret where the devil feeds;
A little flop on Rue St. Paul; an alley
For the damned. He tries to pray.
But it's no good: The French are dead.
It's 1926. Lost without their war,
Statues and police sulk everywhere.

Without

> *"Where knowledge and desire ends,*
> *There is darkness, and there God shines."*
> —Meister Eckhart

Upon his stroke, he did without. Still
He found that he could think, lacking words.
Seeing it, he could think a wooden table,

A glass, its dusty water, its blue,
Unsinkable stars. What spoke to him? He didn't
Think the names. He had to listen. Like an ache

Far into the yard and to the neighbor's yard
And to the neighbor's neighbor's even cows
As dark as hammers flickered in that self-

Same cloud. Twilight, they and all the lights
Would fade. No sense could hold the cows,
Their figures indistinguishable from the land,

In the same late angles as the land, when
He knew: This is God thinking. But he was
Thinking it without. Without *This. God.*

Our Secret Icarus Is

A railway conductor
Who sells coffee on the side.

He should be demanding the tickets.
He should be
Scolding his passengers
Who floundered at the station
With their goodbyes.
He should be pulling them in by the arms.

Ladies and gentlemen
Let's drink a little Russian vodka and be patient now.
He's on his way with a hole in his pocket
And no change
Ringing his little bell.

His cups of coffee are soily grinds.
He spills them handing them over.
He can't interpret what's left
At the bottom of the cup
As a sign.

The math, he says,
Is beyond him.

Lorca's Passport

In the photograph,
Which we know
The poet admired,
Which we know
He called *spiritualistic,*
The vague,
Spotted bow tie
Like a moth
Has come to rest
Slightly crooked
At his throat.
His shirt glows,

The visible portion
An upside-down
Triangle or a lily
That has opened
To bear his head
From the dark
Of the charcoal
Buttoned suit.
One eye
Is shadowed. One ear
Is black, sucked
Into his hair.

The ear we can see
Is a luminous egg.
There is a pinprick
In the center.
The other eye's socket
Swallows his pupil
Like a moat. "It borders
On the light
Of murder,"
He once wrote of it,
"Over my shoulder,
A sort of harp . . ."

Mother, Father

A man on a telephone pole,
The VICTORY banner clutched in one hand,
The hammer in the other, but the banner falls

An inch too short: my mother believes
This first memory is typical for my father,
Our dear pessimist, for whom nothing
Can ever end quite right. Hers is simpler:

She escapes into the alley on Cherry Street,
Where a stranger takes a common hatpin
From a haberdasher's box, and he glares at it in the sun.

View from Inside

To teach me how to use the scythe,
Standa held his two hands over mine.
Beside my body
He guided our bodies
Through the high grass.
Like this.

By dark we had made a little clearing.
You're doing very well, he said.
I couldn't see a thing.
I kept looking up ahead
And swinging,
Like I do this.

Notes

The phrase "Love wants to be sadness" comes from the journals of Padre Pio.

The phrase "Departure's Particular Handkerchief" comes from Ben Belitt's translation of Lorca's *Poet in New York*.

The quotations from "Lorca's Passport" come from his letter to Carlos Morla Lynch, translated by Christopher Maurer.

Acknowledgments

Some of the poems in this manuscript appeared as earlier versions in the following journals:

American Literary Review: "The Sun," "Waking On the Pribor Train, Near Freud's Birthplace"

Gettysburg Review: "Cortez Arrives at San Juan de Ulloa" (as "Cortez")

Intervention: "Elegy for the Precious Time Before Dinner"

Mid-American Review: "Instructions for the Lost" (as "Fable for Jarda")

Ploughshares: "Side Work"

Poetry: "Clocks Kept Upside Down to Stay Awake" (as "Making Arrangements")

Prairie Schooner: "Towards a Reconciliation with Disorder"

Spoon River Poetry Review: "Lorca's Passport," "Further Entries from the Notebook of Anton Chekhov"

The Virginia Quarterly Review: "View from Outside" (as "Stone"), "Justice"

Whiskey Island Magazine: "The Twins Conjoined at the Head Receive Holy Communion at Corpus Christi Church"

Special thanks to grants and fellowships from the National Endowment for the Arts, the Pennsylvania Council on the Arts, and the SOROS Foundation, which aided in the completion of this manuscript, as well as to Jane, Jen K., Jake, Aaron, Rebecca, and Jen R., who inspired many of these poems.

photo by Tim McGettigan

David Keplinger's first book, *The Rose Inside,* won the 1999 T.S. Eliot Prize. His essays, translations, and poems have appeared in *Poetry, Prairie Schooner, Ploughshares, Gettysburg Review, Agni, Green Mountains Review, Virginia Quarterly Review, Mid-American Review, The American Voice,* and many other journals. He has received grants and awards from the National Endowment for the Arts, the Academy of American Poets, the Pennsylvania Council on the Arts, and elsewhere. Keplinger currently directs the Creative Writing Program at Colorado State University–Pueblo.

New Issues Poetry & Prose

Editor, Herbert Scott

Vito Aiuto, *Self-Portrait as Jerry Quarry*
James Armstrong, *Monument in a Summer Hat*
Claire Bateman, *Clumsy*
Maria Beig, *Hermine: An Animal Life* (fiction)
Kevin Boyle, *A Home for Wayward Girls*
Michael Burkard, *Pennsylvania Collection Agency*
Christopher Bursk, *Ovid at Fifteen*
Anthony Butts, *Fifth Season*
Anthony Butts, *Little Low Heaven*
Kevin Cantwell, *Something Black in the Green Part of Your Eye*
Gladys Cardiff, *A Bare Unpainted Table*
Kevin Clark, *In the Evening of No Warning*
Cynie Cory, *American Girl*
Peter Covino, *Cut Off the Ears of Winter*
Jim Daniels, *Night with Drive-By Shooting Stars*
Joseph Featherstone, *Brace's Cove*
Lisa Fishman, *The Deep Heart's Core Is a Suitcase*
Robert Grunst, *The Smallest Bird in North America*
Paul Guest, *The Resurrection of the Body and the Ruin of the World*
Robert Haight, *Emergences and Spinner Falls*
Mark Halperin, *Time as Distance*
Myronn Hardy, *Approaching the Center*
Brian Henry, *Graft*
Edward Haworth Hoeppner, *Rain Through High Windows*
Cynthia Hogue, *Flux*
Christine Hume, *Alaskaphrenia*
Janet Kauffman, *Rot* (fiction)
Josie Kearns, *New Numbers*
David Keplinger, *The Clearing*
Maurice Kilwein Guevara, *Autobiography of So-and-So: Poems in Prose*
Ruth Ellen Kocher, *When the Moon Knows You're Wandering*
Ruth Ellen Kocher, *One Girl Babylon*
Gerry LaFemina, *The Window Facing Winter*
Steve Langan, *Freezing*
Lance Larsen, *Erasable Walls*
David Dodd Lee, *Abrupt Rural*
David Dodd Lee, *Downsides of Fish Culture*
M.L. Liebler, *The Moon a Box*
Deanne Lundin, *The Ginseng Hunter's Notebook*
Barbara Maloutas, *In a Combination of Practices*
Joy Manesiotis, *They Sing to Her Bones*
Sarah Mangold, *Household Mechanics*

Gail Martin, *The Hourglass Heart*
David Marlatt, *A Hog Slaughtering Woman*
Louise Mathias, *Lark Apprentice*
Gretchen Mattox, *Buddha Box*
Gretchen Mattox, *Goodnight Architecture*
Paula McLain, *Less of Her*
Sarah Messer, *Bandit Letters*
Malena Mörling, *Ocean Avenue*
Julie Moulds, *The Woman with a Cubed Head*
Gerald Murnane, *The Plains* (fiction)
Marsha de la O, *Black Hope*
C. Mikal Oness, *Water Becomes Bone*
Bradley Paul, *The Obvious*
Elizabeth Powell, *The Republic of Self*
Margaret Rabb, *Granite Dives*
Rebecca Reynolds, *Daughter of the Hangnail*
Rebecca Reynolds, *The Bovine Two-Step*
Martha Rhodes, *Perfect Disappearance*
Beth Roberts, *Brief Moral History in Blue*
John Rybicki, *Traveling at High Speeds* (expanded second edition)
Mary Ann Samyn, *Inside the Yellow Dress*
Mary Ann Samyn, *Purr*
Ever Saskya, *The Porch is a Journey Different From the House*
Mark Scott, *Tactile Values*
Hugh Seidman, *Somebody Stand Up and Sing*
Martha Serpas, *Côte Blanche*
Diane Seuss-Brakeman, *It Blows You Hollow*
Elaine Sexton, *Sleuth*
Marc Sheehan, *Greatest Hits*
Sarah Jane Smith, *No Thanks—and Other Stories* (fiction)
Heidi Lynn Staples, *Guess Can Gallop*
Phillip Sterling, *Mutual Shores*
Angela Sorby, *Distance Learning*
Matthew Thorburn, *Subject to Change*
Russell Thorburn, *Approximate Desire*
Rodney Torreson, *A Breathable Light*
Robert VanderMolen, *Breath*
Martin Walls, *Small Human Detail in Care of National Trust*
Patricia Jabbeh Wesley, *Before the Palm Could Bloom: Poems of Africa*